PUFFIN  LITTLE

Little
Cook

PUFFIN BOOKS

UK | USA | Canada | Ireland | Australia
India | New Zealand | South Africa | China

Penguin Random House Australia is part of the Penguin Random House group of companies
whose addresses can be found at global.penguinrandomhouse.com.

First published by Puffin Books, an imprint of Penguin Random House Australia Pty Ltd, in 2020

Printed in China

 A catalogue record for this
book is available from the
National Library of Australia

ISBN 978 1 76 089700 0

penguin.com.au

PUFFIN 🐦 LITTLE

Snacks

PUFFIN BOOKS

HELLO, LITTLE COOKS

WELCOME TO MY KITCHEN...

You've popped by at the perfect time. I'm about to get some delicious snacks out of the oven!

The kitchen is one of the busiest places in the house and it's where Big Cooks make breakfast, lunch and dinner every day. Now that you're a Little Cook you're ready to put your hands to work and make some meals of your very own!

We might be LITTLE, but we've got some **BIG** recipes to learn.

Are you ready?

Then turn the page . . .

HOW TO USE THIS BOOK

Before we get started, make sure you read the next few pages with a Big Cook.

All the recipes I've included are my favourite little snacks. There are snacks you can make for breakfast, lunch and dinner. And as a treat, I've added a very special chapter for some delicious **SWEET SNACKS!**

Cooking can be dangerous!

We are Little Cooks and we must learn

from Big Cooks, so when the steps in the recipe

are **orange** or white, you need to

ask a Big Cook to help you.

The tools you need for each recipe can be found on the ingredients page here:

TOOLS:

SERVES
2

And this symbol tells you how much the recipe will make or how many people it will serve.

You'll also see a **Little Tips and Tricks** box on some pages, where you can find alternative ingredients to try out. Have fun and experiment with different flavours!

Now we need to learn some very important **RULES** that will keep us **SAFE** in the kitchen ...

KITCHEN RULES

As Little Cooks we need to learn some **BIG SAFETY RULES** before we get started in the kitchen.

1   Ask a Big Cook's permission before cooking.

2   Wash your hands before you prepare food.

3   Keep countertops and work surfaces clean.

4   Use oven mitts when handling anything hot.

5   Be careful with knives! Ask a Big Cook to help you slice and chop food.

6   Don't lick your fingers when working with raw foods such as cookie dough and meat.

7   **LISTEN, LISTEN, LISTEN!** Always listen to your Big Cook in the kitchen.

LITTLE TOOLS

Big Cooks use lots of different tools in the kitchen. Here are the tools we will be using for our snack recipes ...

CHOPPING AND SLICING

Most recipes will use safety scissors. For any other chopping make sure your Big Cook helps you.

 cheese grater

 safety scissors

 knife

MEASURING AND WEIGHING

We use these tools to work out how much of each ingredient we need.

 measuring cups & spoons

 measuring jug

 scales

COOKING

Always make sure a Big Cook helps you with the OVEN, STOVETOP, MICROWAVE and TOASTER.

toaster	saucepan	microwave	frying pan

EXTRA TOOLS

These tools are for SIFTING, MASHING, ROLLING, BAKING and BLENDING.

potato masher   rolling pin   blender   sieve   hand blender

mixing bowls   baking trays

THE FOOD PYRAMID

Being a Little Cook isn't just about making yummy things to eat, we also need to understand what foods we should eat. Knowing this will help us cook delicious and **HEALTHY** snacks.

The Food Pyramid is our handy guide . . . Down the bottom are the foods we need lots of. And up the top are the foods we should only eat small amounts of.

We should eat:

5–7 SERVINGS A DAY	3–5 SERVINGS A DAY	3 SERVINGS A DAY	2 SERVINGS A DAY	SMALL AMOUNTS	NOT EVERY DAY
FRUIT and VEG	GRAINS bread, potato, pasta	DAIRY milk, cheese, yoghurt	MEAT and PROTEIN	FATS and OILS	Foods high in sugar, salt and fat

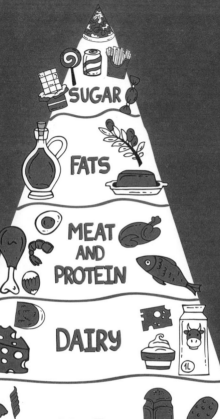

SUGAR

FATS

MEAT AND PROTEIN

DAIRY

GRAINS

FRUIT AND VEG

ARE YOU READY TO MAKE LOTS OF SCRUMPTIOUS SNACKS?

THEN LET'S GET COOKING!

LITTLE
BREAKFAST
SNACKS

· · · · · · · · · · · · · ·

OATMEAL BREAKFAST SMOOTHIE

This delicious little snack will fill up your belly before school.

TOOLS:

INGREDIENTS:

- ¼ cup rolled oats
- ½ cup plain Greek yoghurt
- ½ banana
- ¾ cup frozen mango
- ¾ cup frozen strawberries
- ¾ cup of milk (dairy or non-dairy)

LET'S GET COOKING!

1   Find all the ingredients and measure the correct quantities.

2   Once everything is ready, pop all the ingredients in the blender.

3   **If you need any help, remember to ask a Big Cook to give you a hand.**

4   Blend until smooth.

5   Pour into a glass and drink up before you head off to school!

LITTLE TIPS AND TRICKS

Change up the ingredients and pack this

smoothie full of your favourite fruits!

DIPPY EGGS AND VEGEMITE SOLDIERS

This is a super easy breakfast snack for
Little Cooks to make for the whole family.

TOOLS:

INGREDIENTS:

- 2 eggs
- 2 slices toast, buttered
- 2 teaspoons Vegemite

LET'S GET COOKING!

1 Place the eggs in a saucepan.

2 Add enough water to cover the eggs.

3 **Ask a Big Cook to bring the water to a boil and simmer for 5 minutes.**

4 Spread toast with Vegemite and cut into 2 cm fingers to make soldiers.

5 Place the eggs in egg cups and crack them open.

DUNK THE SOLDIERS IN YOUR EGGS

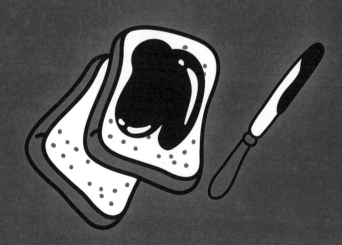

CHOCOLATE COCONUT PORRIDGE

Porridge with coconut is perfect for a healthy breakfast snack. Why not give it a try!

TOOLS:

SERVES 3

INGREDIENTS:

- 2 cups rolled oats
- 3 cups milk (dairy or non-dairy)
- I tablespoon cocoa powder
- I tablespoon shredded coconut
- sliced banana to top

LET'S GET COOKING!

1   Add the oats, milk, cocoa powder and shredded coconut to a saucepan.

2   **With the help of a Big Cook place the saucepan on the stove and cook over a low to medium heat for 5 minutes – stirring occasionally.**

3   You will know when the oats are cooked because all the milk will have been absorbed.

4   Spoon the porridge into bowls and top with a sprinkling of coconut and some banana slices.

YUMMY

LITTLE TIPS AND TRICKS

Make this breakfast snack
even more delicious and
add a drizzle of maple
syrup.

ENERGY BALL BITES

These little bites are a brilliant breakfast snack for on the go. Make them in the evening and enjoy them the next morning!

TOOLS:

MAKES
32

INGREDIENTS:

- 1½ cups rolled oats
- 1½ cups crispy rice cereal
- ½ cup shredded coconut
- ¼ cup chia seeds
- ¼ cup flaxseed (ground)
- ¼ cup mini chocolate chips
- ½ cup peanut butter
- ¼ cup coconut oil
- ¼ cup honey

LET'S GET COOKING!

1   Find all the ingredients and measure the correct quantities.

2   In a large mixing bowl, combine all the dry ingredients.

3   In a small mixing bowl, stir together the peanut butter, coconut oil and honey until smooth.

4   Pour the peanut butter mixture over the dry ingredients and stir together.

5   Place the mixture in the fridge to chill for 20–40 minutes.

6 Once chilled, press 2 tablespoons of mixture together and roll into small balls.

7 Place all your energy balls in a container and store in the fridge – ready for a **GRAB 'N' GO** breakfast snack!

LITTLE LUNCH SNACKS

GUACAMOLE AND TORTILLA DIPPERS

This is a great little lunch snack as avocados are not only yummy but they are **FULL** of vitamins.

INGREDIENTS:

GUACAMOLE

- 2 ripe avocados
- handful of fresh coriander
- 1 teaspoon lemon juice
- pinch of salt

TORTILLA DIPPERS

- 2 plain wraps
- olive oil

LET'S GET COOKING!

GUACAMOLE

1 **With the help of a Big Cook halve the avocados and remove the stones.**

2 Using a spoon, scoop out the flesh of the avocado into a shallow bowl.

3 Mash with a potato masher or fork until smooth.

4 Cut up the coriander with a pair of safety scissors.

5 Add in the coriander, lemon juice and salt and stir together.

TORTILLA DIPPERS

1 **Ask a Big Cook to preheat the oven to 180°C.**

2 Cut the tortilla wraps into triangles with a pair of safety scissors and lay on a baking tray.

3 **Brush with oil and ask a Big Cook to bake the wraps for 5 minutes.**

4 Let the tortilla dippers cool once out of the oven and then serve up with your **TASTY GUACAMOLE!**

TOMATO AND BASIL PINWHEEL SANDWICHES

Liven up your lunch box with these
scrumptious pinwheel sandwiches.
Everyone will want to try them!

INGREDIENTS:

- ½ cup sun-dried tomatoes

- 225 grams cream cheese

- ¼ cup spinach

- ¼ cup parmesan cheese, grated

- pinch of salt

- 2 whole-wheat tortillas

- 15 basil leaves

LET'S GET COOKING!

1   Cut up the sun-dried tomatoes into small pieces using a pair of safety scissors. Watch your fingers!

2   Mix the sun-dried tomatoes in a bowl with the cream cheese, spinach, grated parmesan cheese and salt.

3   Get your tortillas and spread the cream cheese filling all the way to the edges.

4   Sprinkle the basil leaves over the top and roll up the tortilla tightly.

5 **Ask a Big Cook to slice the roll into pieces, roughly 2–3 cm thick.**

LITTLE TIPS AND TRICKS

When cutting the roll, keep the open
edge facedown against the bench to help
it stay closed.

VEGGIE PIKELETS

These delicious veggie treats can be tricky to make. Always ask a **Big Cook** to lend a helping hand.

TOOLS:

MAKES
12

INGREDIENTS:

- 1 onion, peeled and grated
- 1 carrot, peeled and grated
- 1 zucchini, peeled and grated
- 1 cup capsicum, grated
- 1 tablespoon oil
- 1 tablespoon cheese, grated
- 1 cup white self-raising flour
- ½ cup wholemeal self-raising flour
- 1 egg, beaten
- 1½ cups milk

LET'S GET COOKING!

1   **With the help of a Big Cook peel and grate all the vegetables.**

2   **Ask a Big Cook to heat the oil in a frying pan. Add the onion and cook until softened. Remove from the heat and set aside.**

3   Sift the flours into a large mixing bowl. Add the cheese, cooked onion, carrot, zucchini and capsicum and mix together until combined. You can even do the mixing with your hands!

4   Make a well in the centre of the mixture. Add the beaten egg and milk. Mix to form a smooth batter.

5 **Ask a Big Cook to heat the frying pan over a low heat and add a little more oil.**

6 Carefully place 2 tablespoons of the mixture into the pan for each pikelet.

7 Cook until brown and then flip over to cook the other side. Remember to ask a Big Cook for help when you need it!

LITTLE TIPS AND TRICKS

These tasty veggie treats can be served hot or cold!

LITTLE PEA FRITTATAS

These little frittatas are great for your school lunch box. **DELICIOUS!**

TOOLS:

INGREDIENTS:

- butter for greasing
- 4 eggs
- 1 spring onion
- ½ cup feta cheese
- ¾ cup peas

LET'S GET COOKING!

1   Ask a **Big Cook** to preheat the oven to 180°C.

2   Dip a piece of paper towel in some butter and grease the holes in the muffin tray.

3   Crack the eggs into a measuring jug and beat together with a fork.

4   Cut up the spring onion into little pieces using a pair of safety scissors. Add to the egg mixture.

5   Crumble up the feta cheese with your fingers and add it to the mixture.

6   Mix everything together then pour the mixture into the muffin tray. Sprinkle the peas into each of the holes.

7   **Ask a Big Cook to bake the frittatas in the oven for 12–15 minutes.**

8   **Remove from the oven and with the help of a Big Cook pop the pea frittatas out of the muffin tray.**

LITTLE TIPS AND TRICKS

If you don't like feta cheese why not try grated cheddar or parmesan instead?

LITTLE DINNER SNACKS

PIZZA SCROLLS   58

SAUSAGE AND ZUCCHINI
KEBABS   62

CHUNKY
FISH FINGERS   66

TASTY TOMATO
SOUP   70

LITTLE DINNER SNACKS

PIZZA SCROLLS

Who doesn't love pizza?!
These scrummy pizza scrolls are a quick
and easy dinner snack.

MAKES 8

INGREDIENTS:

- 2 cups Greek yoghurt
- 2 cups self-raising flour
- 1 cup tomato sauce (passata)
- 2 cups mozzarella cheese, grated
- 1 tablespoon Italian herbs
- oil for greasing

LET'S GET COOKING!

1   Ask your **Big Cook** to preheat the oven to 190°C.

2   Dip a piece of paper towel in some olive oil and grease the baking tray.

3   In a large bowl, combine the yoghurt and flour. Use your hands and mix together until you have made a soft ball.

4   Sprinkle a small amount of flour on a clean surface then knead the dough for 5 minutes. Add extra flour if it's too sticky.

5   Roll out the dough into a large rectangle of even thickness.

6   Spread tomato sauce over the entire dough surface. Use the back of a tablespoon to spread it out evenly.

7   Sprinkle cheese on top of the tomato sauce and shake over the Italian herbs.

8   **Roll the dough into a log. Ask a Big Cook to slice into 2 cm pieces and place on the baking tray.**

9   **Sprinkle with a little more cheese and with the help of a Big Cook bake in the oven for 20–25 minutes.**

SAUSAGE AND ZUCCHINI KEBABS

These FUN-tastic kebabs will be gobbled up

as soon as they are served.

INGREDIENTS:

- 2 zucchinis, cut into chunks
- ½ yellow capsicum, cut into fat strips
- 3 sausages
- 8 cherry tomatoes
- oil, for brushing

LET'S GET COOKING!

1 **Ask a Big Cook to preheat the oven to 200°C.**

2 Cut the zucchinis and capsicum into chunks with your safety scissors or ask a Big Cook to help.

3 Now cut each sausage into 3 or 4 pieces with your scissors, or you could ask your Big Cook to do this with a knife.

4 Push the kebab sticks through the cherry tomatoes, capsicums, zucchini and pieces of sausage in any order. Make sure the sharp end of the kebab stick is pointing away from you.

5   Brush your skewers with olive oil and place on a baking tray.

6   **Ask a Big Cook to put the kebabs in the oven for 20 minutes, or until the vegetables are soft and the sausage is cooked.**

LITTLE TIPS AND TRICKS

You could ask your Big Cook to grill these kebabs on the barbecue!

CHUNKY FISH FINGERS

These homemade chunky, crispy fish fingers are super yummy. Make sure you eat them with lots of green veggies.

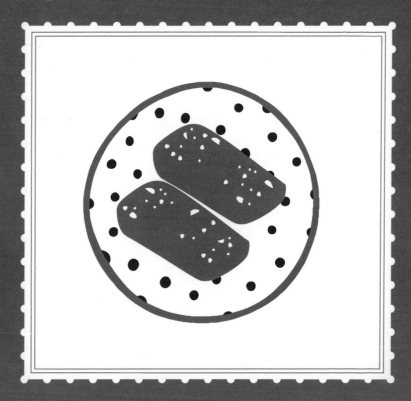

TOOLS:

MAKES 10

INGREDIENTS:

- 500 grams skinless, boneless chunky white fish fillet, cut into bite size chunks
- 1 cup plain flour
- 3 large eggs, beaten
- 2 cups dried breadcrumbs
- pinch of salt
- olive oil

LET'S GET COOKING!

1 **Ask a Big Cook to preheat the oven to 200°C.**

2 Brush some olive oil all over the baking tray.

3 Place 3 bowls on your work surface. Fill one with the flour, one with the beaten eggs and one with the breadcrumbs.

4 Place your baking tray next to the bowls, ready for the uncooked fish fingers.

5 Using your hands, dip the fish in the flour.
Give it a shake and then dunk it in the egg.
Finally, roll the fish in the breadcrumbs so it's
completely coated and place the fish on the
baking tray. Repeat with all the fish chunks.

6 **Ask a Big Cook to put the fish fingers
in the oven and cook for 10–12 minutes,
or until golden. Turn them over halfway
through cooking so both sides are crispy.**

TASTY TOMATO SOUP

Big dinners for the whole family can be tricky to make, but this tasty tomato soup is super simple!

TOOLS:

SERVES
4

INGREDIENTS:

- 2 tablespoons olive oil
- I onion, peeled and chopped
- 2 carrots, peeled and chopped
- I garlic clove, crushed
- 800 grams vine tomatoes, chopped and squished
- 400 grams can of plum tomatoes
- 3 cups vegetable stock

LET'S GET COOKING!

1 With the help of a **Big Cook** peel and chop the onion and the carrots.

2 Ask a **Big Cook** to heat the oil in a large pan over a medium heat.

3 Add the onion and carrot to the pan, reduce the heat to low and cook for 10–15 minutes. Make sure you stir regularly.

4 Using a garlic crusher, crush the garlic and add to the pan. Cook for another minute.

5   Now it's time to get your hands dirty! Chop up
    the vine tomatoes and place them in a mixing
    bowl. Using your hands give them a good squish.

6   Add the squished vine tomatoes, plum tomatoes
    and the stock to the pan.

7   **Ask a Big Cook to bring the soup to the boil, then
    reduce the heat and simmer for 25 minutes.**

8   With a hand blender, blend the soup until nice
    and smooth.

LITTLE
SWEET
SNACKS

· · · · · · · · · · · · · · ·

RAINBOW FRUIT SKEWERS

These vitamin-packed fruit skewers are a simple, colourful and fun way to get your FIVE A DAY!

TOOLS:

MAKES
7

INGREDIENTS:

- ○ **7 raspberries**
- ○ **7 strawberries**
- ○ **7 orange segments**
- ○ **7 mango cubes**
- ○ **7 pineapple chunks**
- ○ **7 kiwifruit chunks**
- ○ **7 green grapes**
- ○ **7 red grapes**
- ○ **14 blueberries**

LET'S GET COOKING!

1 **Ask a Big Cook to help you with the chopping and peeling.**

2 Take 7 wooden skewers and thread the following fruit onto each:

* * **1 raspberry**
* * **1 strawberry**
* * **1 orange segment**
* * **1 cube of mango**
* * **1 chunk of pineapple**
* * **1 chunk of kiwifruit**
* * **1 green grape**
* * **1 red grape**
* * **2 blueberries**

FRUIT IS DELICIOUS

LITTLE TIPS AND TRICKS

You can try out lots of different fruit combinations. Stick to your favourites or try something new!

FROZEN BANANA POPS

These sweet snacks are sure to hit the spot!
They are super easy to make and you can
cover them with your favourite toppings.

TOOLS:

INGREDIENTS:

- 3 medium bananas
- 1 cup chocolate chips

TOPPINGS:
(choose your favourites)

- chia seeds
- shredded coconut
- sesame seeds

LITTLE SWEET SNACKS

LET'S GET COOKING!

1   Cut each banana into 6 pieces using your safety scissors. Take a paddle pop stick and insert it in the centre of each banana pop.

2   Place all your banana pops on a tray lined with baking paper and put in the freezer for 1 hour.

3   **With the help of a Big Cook, melt the chocolate chips in the microwave.**

4   Now for the fun part! Dip each banana pop in the melted chocolate, then sprinkle with your favourite toppings.

5 Return your banana pops to the tray lined with baking paper and freeze for 30 minutes before serving.

LITTLE TIPS AND TRICKS

To make these banana pops even healthier, dip them in yoghurt instead of chocolate.

FRUIT SLUSHIE

Healthy and refreshing!
This slushie is full of fruity goodness and is
the perfect treat for summer afternoons.

TOOLS:

MAKES
6

INGREDIENTS:

- ○ **2 cups watermelon, chopped**
- ○ **2 cups rockmelon, chopped**
- ○ **2 cups honeydew melon, chopped**

LITTLE SWEET SNACKS

LET'S GET COOKING!

1   Chop up all the melons with a **Big Cook** and measure out 2 cups of each.

2   Next, with the help of a **Big Cook**, blitz the watermelon in a blender until smooth. Pour into a shallow container. Rinse the blender and repeat with the rockmelon, then the honeydew. Put all the containers in the freezer overnight.

3   When you are ready to serve up your slushies, remove the 3 containers from the freezer and set aside for 20 minutes to thaw slightly.

4   Mash up the frozen melons with a fork.

5   To serve, spoon layers of the watermelon,

rockmelon and honeydew into a smoothie cup.

A
REFRESHING
SUMMER TREAT

ANZAC BISCUITS

These sweet snacks are called Anzac biscuits because they were shipped to the Anzac soldiers during World War One.

TOOLS:

MAKES 20

INGREDIENTS:

- 1 cup plain flour
- 1 cup brown sugar
- 1 cup rolled oats
- ½ cup shredded coconut
- 125 grams butter
- 2 tablespoons golden syrup
- 1 tablespoon water
- ½ teaspoon bicarbonate of soda

LITTLE SWEET SNACKS

LET'S GET COOKING!

1   Before you get started make sure you ask a **Big Cook** to preheat the oven to 175°C.

2   Sift the flour into a bowl, then add the sugar, rolled oats and shredded coconut.

3   With the help of a **Big Cook** melt the butter in a saucepan, then add the golden syrup and water.

4   Stir the bicarbonate of soda into the liquid mixture.

5   Add the liquid to the dry ingredients and mix thoroughly.

6 Scoop out little handfuls of the mixture and shape them into small balls.

7 **Place them on a greased baking tray and ask a Big Cook to bake them at 175°C for 15–20 minutes.**

DUNK THEM IN YOUR TEA

GLOSSARY

BAKE: to cook food in an oven.

BEAT: to whisk or stir something to combine, thicken or aerate.

BLEND: to mix ingredients together with a spoon, fork or food blender.

BOIL: to heat a food so that the liquid gets hot enough for bubbles to rise and break the surface.

CHOP: to cut into small pieces.

COOK: to prepare food for a meal.

GRATE: to scrape food against the holes of a grater making thin pieces.

GREASE: to lightly coat with oil or butter so food does not stick when cooking or baking.

INGREDIENTS: a list of food items to be used in a recipe.

KNEAD: to press and fold dough until it is smooth. Usually done with the heels of your hands.

MASH: to squash food with a fork, potato masher or your hands.

MIX: to stir ingredients together with a spoon or fork until well combined.

PEEL: to strip off the skin or rind of a fruit or vegetable.

PREHEAT: to heat an oven to the desired temperature before using.

RECIPE: a step-by-step guide to creating a meal.

TOOLS: a list of instruments to be used in a recipe.

PUFFIN QUIZ

1. How many servings of **FRUIT** and **VEG** should we have each day?

2. What should we do before handling any food?

3. Name **3 FOODS** that are in the **GRAINS** group of the food pyramid.

4. How many servings of **DAIRY** should we have every day?

5. Name **3 FOODS** that we should **NOT** eat every day.

ANSWERS:
1. 5–7 servings 2. wash your hands 3. might include: bread, potato, pasta 4. 3 servings 5. might include: pizza, lollies, chocolate.

A PUFFIN LITTLE BOOK